j745.592 H691t
Hodgson, Harriet W.
Toyworks
   $8.95

LEVI

D1788114

LEVI

Memphis and Shelby County Public Library and Information Center

OCT 27 1986

For the Residents
of
Memphis and Shelby County

BLI

TOYWORKS

By Harriet Hodgson
Illustrated by Beth Savage

Publisher: Roberta Suid
Editor: Elizabeth Russell
Cover Design: David Hale
Design and Production: Susan Pinkerton
Cover Art: Corbin Hillam

ISBN 0-912107-40-5

Monday Morning is a registered trademark
of Monday Morning Books, Inc.

Entire contents copyright © 1986 by Monday Morning
Books, Inc., Box 1680, Palo Alto, California 94302

Permission is hereby granted to reproduce
student materials in this book for non-commercial
individual or classroom use.

Printed in the United States of America

9 8 7 6 5 4 3 2 1

Contents

Introduction	4	Mini-Greenhouse	34
		Moon People	35
Activities		Party Pak	36
Barn and Silo	5	Pencil Pinwheel	37
Big Bucks	6	Pick Up Picks	38
Bookmarks	7	Pilot Control Panel	39
Box Train	8	Plain Plane	40
Bulletin Board	9	Pop Bop	41
Bunny Bank	10	Pop Goes the Clown's Nose	42
Cardboard Castle	11	Rack 'Em, Stack 'Em	43
C.B. Radio	12	Rainbow Book	44
Centipede	13	Rocket	45
Chug Tug	14	Royal Guard	46
Comical Place Mats	15	Small Stuff	47
Cozy Bed	16	Soap Boat	48
Crowned	17	Spongy Blocks	49
Cylinder Soldiers	18	Squirt Tricks	50
Faces and Feelings	19	Stencils and Pencils	51
Farm Animals	20	Stone Age Jewelry	52
Fortune Teller	21	Teddy's Picnic	53
Free Flyer	22	Tip Tops	54
Gas Pumps	23	Toy Town	55
Gingerbread Person	24	Triangle Tents	56
Great Glider	25	T.V. Me	57
Grow Kit	27	U.S. Mail	58
Headphones	28	Wash-Me Mitt	59
Hug Me	29	Wind Chimes	60
Jump Rope	30	Windsock	61
Kitchen Caper	31	Wooden Spoon Doll	62
Knee Desk	32	Wristwatch	63
Marble Maze	33	Yolk-O-Motion	64

Introduction

With *Toyworks,* some imagination, and lots of free materials, any room can become a toy factory. All of the toys in this book are simple enough for children to make themselves out of recycled throwaway materials. Children have twice as much fun with these toys: first in the making and then in the playing.

GATHERING MATERIALS
Collect all kinds of plastic, paper, styrofoam, and cardboard packaging materials. Wash and dry plastic bottles and tubs, shake crumbs from boxes, and fold paper bags. Check all items for safety. Do not use metal cans with sharp edges, containers which once held chemicals, or anything made of glass. Sort all materials and store in a handy place.

MAKING THE TOYS
Before doing any activity with children, make each toy yourself to discover any difficulties with the project. You will also be able to see possibilities for substituting materials or extending the activity.

Have the materials and tools ready before you begin. Nothing is more frustrating than having to stop in the middle of a project to hunt for something.

Show children the basic steps to make a toy, but encourage them to use their imaginations to modify the toys in any way they like.

Use permanent markers in a well-ventilated room. Never allow children to sniff the fumes, as they can cause brain damage.

ENJOYING THE TOYS
The ideas in *Toyworks* are just the beginning of a toy factory. Brainstorm with children new ways to turn trash into toys. Keep looking for unusual throwaways. Challenge children to invent their own playthings with whatever is at hand. They will learn a useful lesson about recycling. More importantly, they will learn that creativity can be the most rewarding form of entertainment.

Barn and Silo

WHAT YOU NEED:
Shoe box
Oatmeal carton
3 pieces of colored paper (2 red, 1 white)
Pencil
White glue
Scissors
Plastic coffee can lid (2-pound size)

WHAT YOU DO:
1. Trace around the sides of the shoe box on red paper, cut out, and glue onto the box.
2. Cut red paper to fit around the oatmeal carton and glue it on.
3. Trace around the coffee can lid on red paper. Cut out this circle and cut halfway through its diameter. Overlap edges to form a cone and glue together. Glue this shape to the bottom of the oatmeal carton for the silo roof.
4. Fold the white paper in half lengthwise, then open it up and fold each side again towards the center crease to make the barn roof. Glue the roof to the shoe box.
5. Cut a barn door in one side of the box.

Big Bucks

WHAT YOU NEED:
2 pieces of green paper
Scissors
Crayons
Envelope

WHAT YOU DO:
1. Fold each piece of paper in half lengthwise, then in half crosswise. Now fold the paper in half again crosswise.
2. Open the paper and cut on the fold lines. These rectangles are paper money.
3. Print a numeral in the center of each bill. Make dollar signs in the corners.
4. Cut the flap off the envelope to make a wallet. Decorate the wallet with crayons and fill it with paper money.

Bookmarks

WHAT YOU NEED:
Colored paper scraps
Scissors
Crayons or watercolor markers
Clear contact paper
Spoon
Paper punch
Yarn

WHAT YOU DO:
1. Cut a small rectangle from colored paper.
2. Draw on both sides with crayons or markers.
3. Cover both sides with clear contact paper, rubbing with the back of a spoon to remove any air bubbles.
4. Trim edges.
5. Punch a hole in the top of the bookmark. Tie on yarn trim. Braid the yarn or make a tassle, if desired.

Box Train

WHAT YOU NEED:
Big boxes (large enough to hold a child)
Cardboard ice cream carton (from ice cream store)
Large brass paper fastener
Nail or nutpick
Scissors
String

WHAT YOU DO:
1. Poke a hole in the center of the bottom of the ice cream carton with a nail or nutpick.
2. Poke a matching hole in the side of one box.
3. Attach the ice cream carton to the box with the brass paper fastener to make the train engine.
4. Punch holes in the short sides of the other boxes.
5. Tie the boxes together, then hitch the box cars to the engine.

Bulletin Board

WHAT YOU NEED:
Large piece of corrugated cardboard
White glue
Scraps of fabric trims
Scissors
Nail or nutpick
Pushpins

WHAT YOU DO:
1. Glue a border of trim around all edges of the cardboard.
2. Cut a long piece of trim for a handle.
3. Punch holes in the upper corners of the cardboard. Tie one end of the handle in each hole.
4. Hang the bulletin board in a convenient place. Post pictures, cards, and notes on bulletin board with pushpins.

Bunny Bank

WHAT YOU NEED:
Clean margarine tub with lid
Permanent marker
Plastic coffee can lid
Scissors
Kitchen shears

WHAT YOU DO:
1. Draw a bunny face on the margarine tub lid with marker.
2. Cut a slit for money along the bunny's mouth.
3. Snap the lid onto the margarine tub.
4. Cut two bunny ears from the coffee can lid.
5. Use kitchen shears to cut two slits in the side of the margarine tub. Slip the ears into these slits.

Cardboard Castle

WHAT YOU NEED:
4 cardboard milk cartons (clean and dry)
Tape
6 cardboard box dividers
Scissors
Brown wrapping paper (or grocery bags)
Glue
Scraps of colored paper
2 spring-type wooden clothespins
Watercolor markers

WHAT YOU DO:
1. Tape milk carton tops closed. Cut four pieces of brown paper 7½" high and wide enough to wrap around the milk cartons. Glue paper on cartons to form towers.
2. Fit four box dividers together like tic-tac-toe lines. Stand a milk carton tower in each corner of the castle.
3. Cut four rectangles from box dividers for tower roofs. Fold rectangles in half and put them on top of the milk cartons as shown.
4. Cut a castle door, leaving ½" between the door and the floor. Add a ramp made from a rectangle of colored paper with one end folded in to attach it to the castle.
5. Cut two flags from scrap paper. Glue a flag to the handle of each clothespin. Snap the flags onto the castle wall.
6. Draw windows and people on the walls with markers.

C.B. Radio

WHAT YOU NEED:
Small saltine box
2 pieces of black paper
Pencil
Scissors
White glue
2 plastic milk bottle tops
Notched plastic trash bag tie
Nail or nutpick
3 brass paper fasteners
Small cardboard juice can
String
Tape

WHAT YOU DO:
1. Trace top and sides of box on black paper. Cut out rectangles and glue to box.
2. Cut black paper to fit around juice can and glue on.
3. Poke holes in the center of the bottle tops with nail or nutpick. Also poke holes in the side of the box for control knobs and arrow.
4. Trim trash bag tie to an arrow shape that fits on the side of the box. Attach knobs and arrow with brass paper fasteners.
5. Cut a piece of string about two feet long. Knot both ends. Slip one end through the end of the box and tape it in place. Tape the other other end to the juice can to make the microphone.

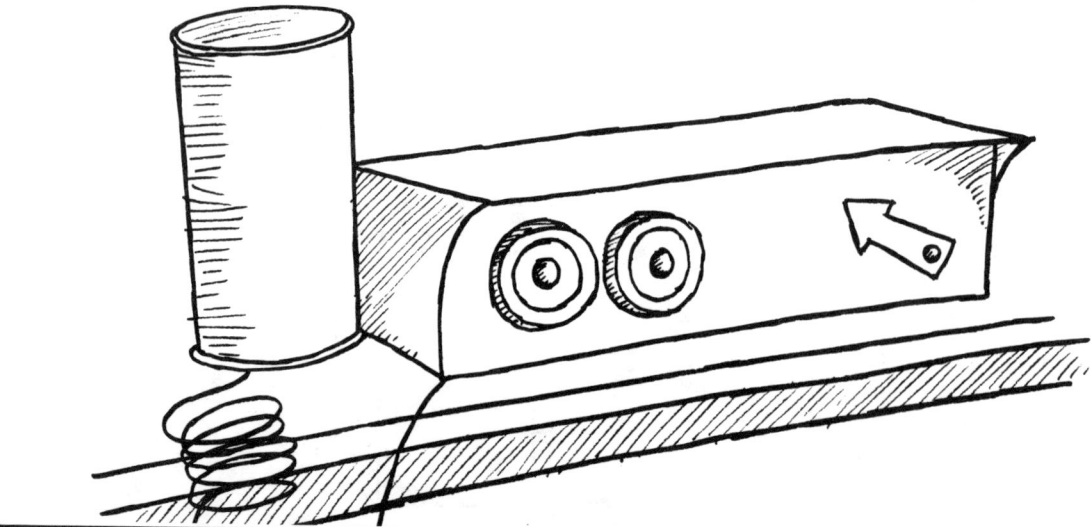

Centipede

WHAT YOU NEED:
Egg carton
Scissors
12 spring-type clothespins
2 pipe cleaners
Ball-point pen

WHAT YOU DO:
1. Cut the top off the egg carton. Save the bottom. If the carton has a locking strip, cut that off, too.
2. Cut the egg carton bottom in half lengthwise.
3. Snap a clothespin onto each bump of each carton half.
4. Coil the pipe cleaners around the pen.
5. Push the coils through one end of the carton to make antennae.
6. Draw two eyes with the pen under the antennae.

Chug Tug

WHAT YOU NEED:
3 egg cartons
2 small pipe cleaners
Toilet paper tube
Tape
Absorbent cotton or polyester stuffing

WHAT YOU DO:
1. Cut off the tops of the egg cartons and save them.
2. Link the tops together with pipe cleaners. Poke pipe cleaners through the short sides and twist them together.
3. Tape the tube onto the first lid near the front to make the tug.
4. Place cotton in the tube for smoke in the tug's smokestack.
5. Fill the barges with small things, such as cars, blocks, or toy soldiers.

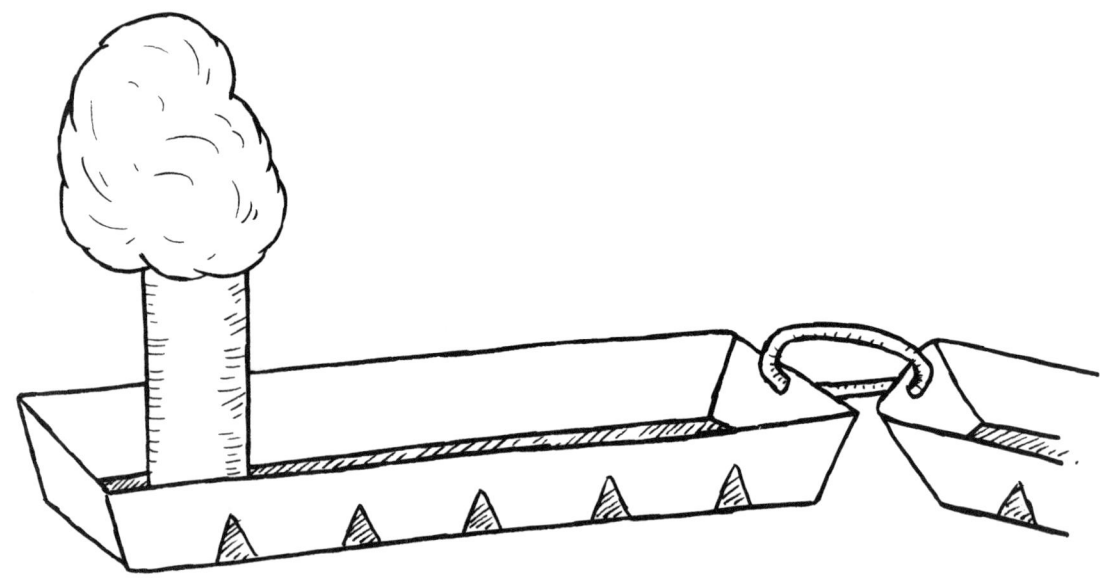

Comical Place Mats

WHAT YOU NEED:
Sunday comics
Piece of typing paper
Pencil
Scissors
Clear contact paper
Spoon
Pinking shears

WHAT YOU DO:
1. Place typing paper over comics, aligning edges, and trace it. Cut out this rectangle.
2. Cut two pieces of clear contact paper slightly larger than the rectangle.
3. Peel off the backing and carefully fit the clear contact paper over the comics. Rub the plastic with the back of the spoon to remove any air bubbles. Repeat this procedure to cover the other side of the comics.
4. Trim the edges of the place mat with pinking shears.

Cozy Bed

WHAT YOU NEED:
Shoe box
Brown paper bag
Pencil
White glue
4 straight wooden clothespins
Bandanna

WHAT YOU DO:
1. Trace the sides of the box onto the paper bag and cut out these four rectangles.
2. Glue paper rectangles to the sides of the box.
3. Stand a clothespin bedpost at each corner of the box.
4. Add the bandanna for a blanket to tuck in a doll, stuffed animal, or teddy bear.

Crowned

WHAT YOU NEED:
Brown paper bag (medium size)
Crayons
Scissors
Paper clip
Old towel (optional)

WHAT YOU DO:
1. Punch out the sides of the paper bag and flatten them.
2. Draw a crown across the width of the bag.
3. Cut out the crown, clipping through both sides of the bag at the same time.
4. Color jewels on the crown.
5. Check the crown for fit. If it is too big, fold over the extra paper and hold it in place with the paper clip.
6. Turn an old towel into a cape to complete the costume, if desired.

Cylinder Soldiers

WHAT YOU NEED:
Toilet paper tubes
Colored paper
Scissors
Paste
Permanent marker

WHAT YOU DO:
1. Cut colored paper to fit around the cardboard tubes.
2. Glue paper onto each tube.
3. Add a face with permanent marker.

Faces and Feelings

WHAT YOU NEED:
Small paper plates
Permanent marker
Scissors
Craft sticks
Glue

WHAT YOU DO:
1. Draw a different facial expression on each paper plate.
2. Cut out the eyes spaces on each plate to make a mask.
3. Glue a craft stick to the bottom of each mask.
4. Hold each mask up and tell a story.

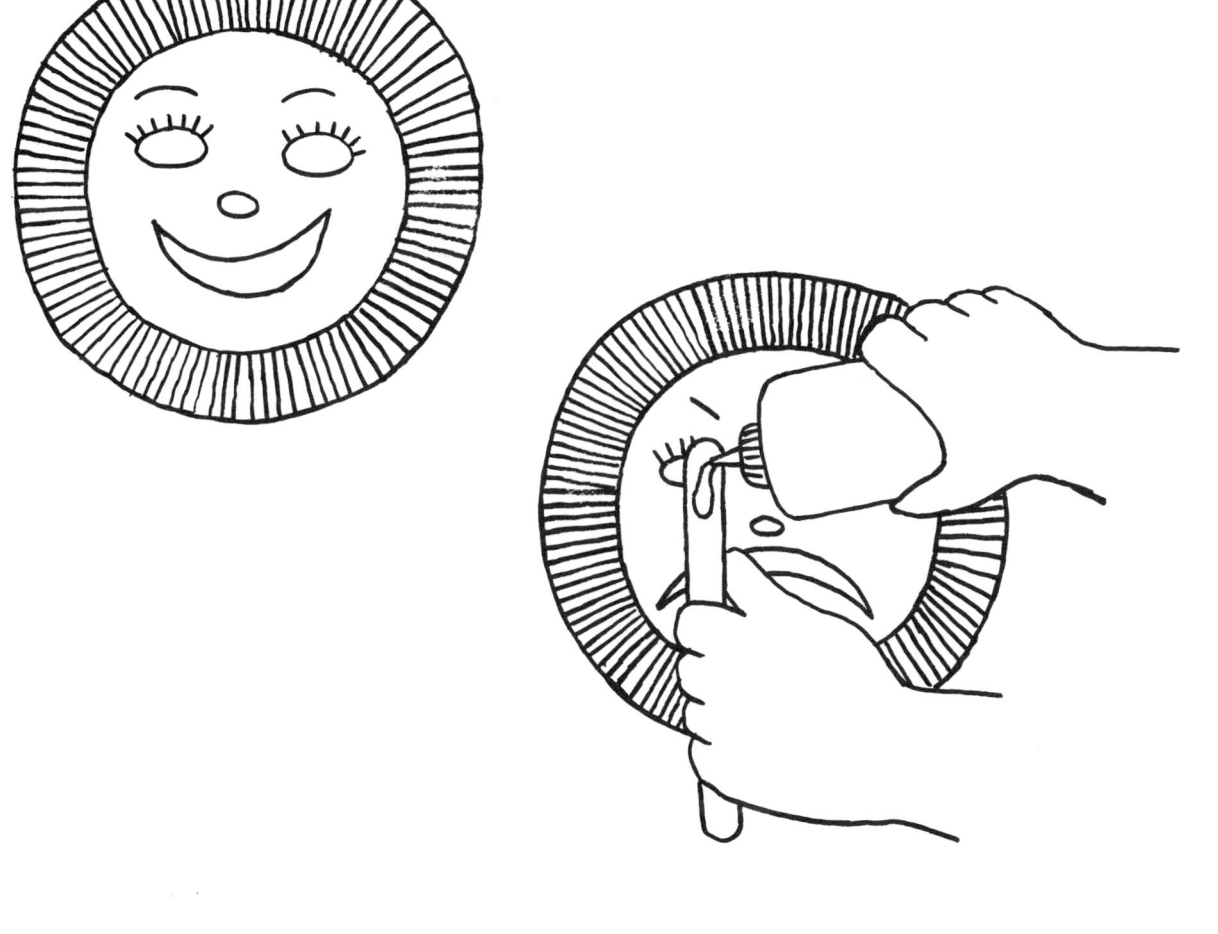

Farm Animals

WHAT YOU NEED:
3" x 5" blank index cards
Crayons
Scissors
Spring-type clothespins

WHAT YOU DO:
1. Draw one farm animal on each index card. Do not draw the animal's legs.
2. Cut out the animals.
3. Snap on clothespin legs to make the animals stand. Use mini travel clothespins for small legs on small animals.

Fortune Teller

WHAT YOU NEED:
Egg carton
Ball-point pen
Small button

WHAT YOU DO:
1. Open the egg carton and print one of these words in the bottom of each cup: yes, no, maybe, none, never, soon, sure, many, few. Also print three question marks.
2. Put the button inside the egg carton and close the lid.
3. Think of a question and shake the carton.
4. Wherever the button lands is the answer to the question. If the button lands on a question mark, shake again.

Free Flyer

WHAT YOU NEED:
Permanent marker
Plastic lid from ice cream bucket

WHAT YOU DO:
1. Decorate the lid with the permanent marker. Swirls make interesting patterns while the flyer sails.
2. Toss the flyer with a flick of the wrist.

Gas Pumps

WHAT YOU NEED:
Shoelace
Scissors
2 toothpaste boxes (same size)
Paper
White glue
Nail or nutpick
Small piece of cardboard

WHAT YOU DO:
1. Cut the shoelace in half. Glue the flat part of each half under the end of each toothpaste box to make a gas hose.
2. Wrap paper around the toothpaste boxes, creasing the corners. Trim paper to fit and glue in place. Also glue small pieces of paper over the ends of the boxes.
3. Poke a hole in the side of each box with a nail or nutpick to hang up the gas hose.
4. Glue the gas pumps onto the piece of cardboard.

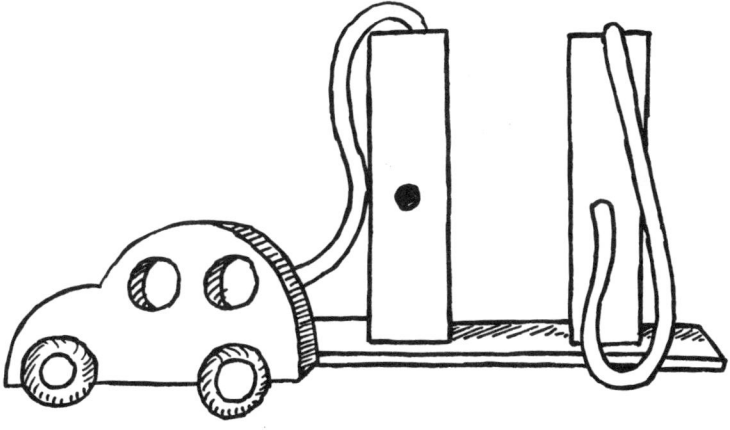

Gingerbread Person

WHAT YOU NEED:
Brown paper bag
Crayons
Scissors
Paper punch
Yarn
Newspaper

WHAT YOU DO:
1. Push out the sides of the bag to flatten them.
2. Draw a gingerbread person on one side of the bag. Cut out the gingerbread person, clipping through both sides of the bag at the same time.
3. Draw a face on one side of the gingerbread person.
4. Punch holes through both thicknesses around the edge of the gingerbread person.
5. Stitch together with yarn, leaving an opening for stuffing.
6. Tear newspaper into small pieces. Stuff the gingerbread person with newspaper and stitch the opening closed.

Great Glider

WHAT YOU NEED:
Styrofoam meat tray
Ball-point pen
Scissors
Large paper clip

WHAT YOU DO:
1. Cut the rims off the long sides of the meat tray.
2. Trace the patterns for the glider body, wing, and tail on the meat tray with ball-point pen. The wing should have rims.
3. Cut out all glider parts.
4. Cut slits in the body to insert wing and tail.
5. Fasten the paper clip to the nose of the glider, letting it protrude a bit. (With a larger meat tray, lengthen the glider body and shorten the clip.)

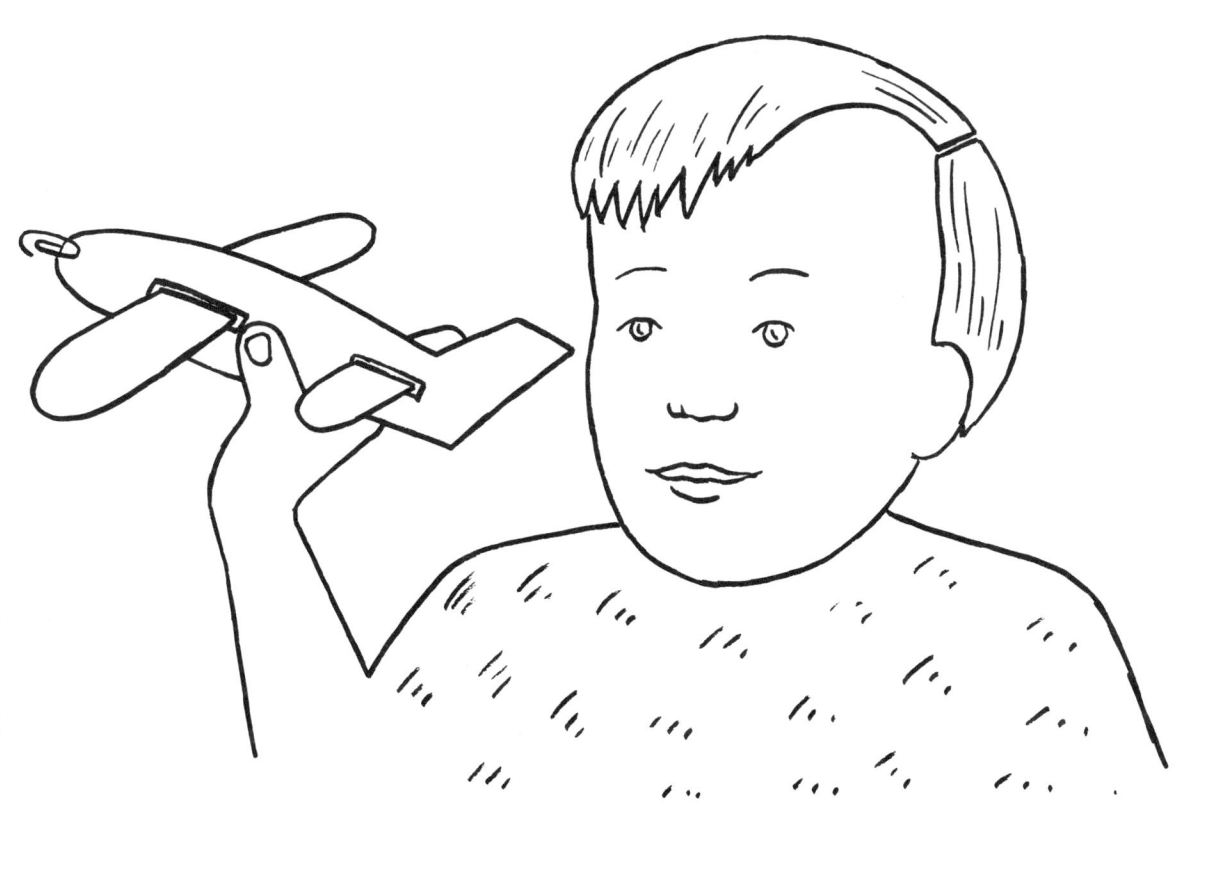

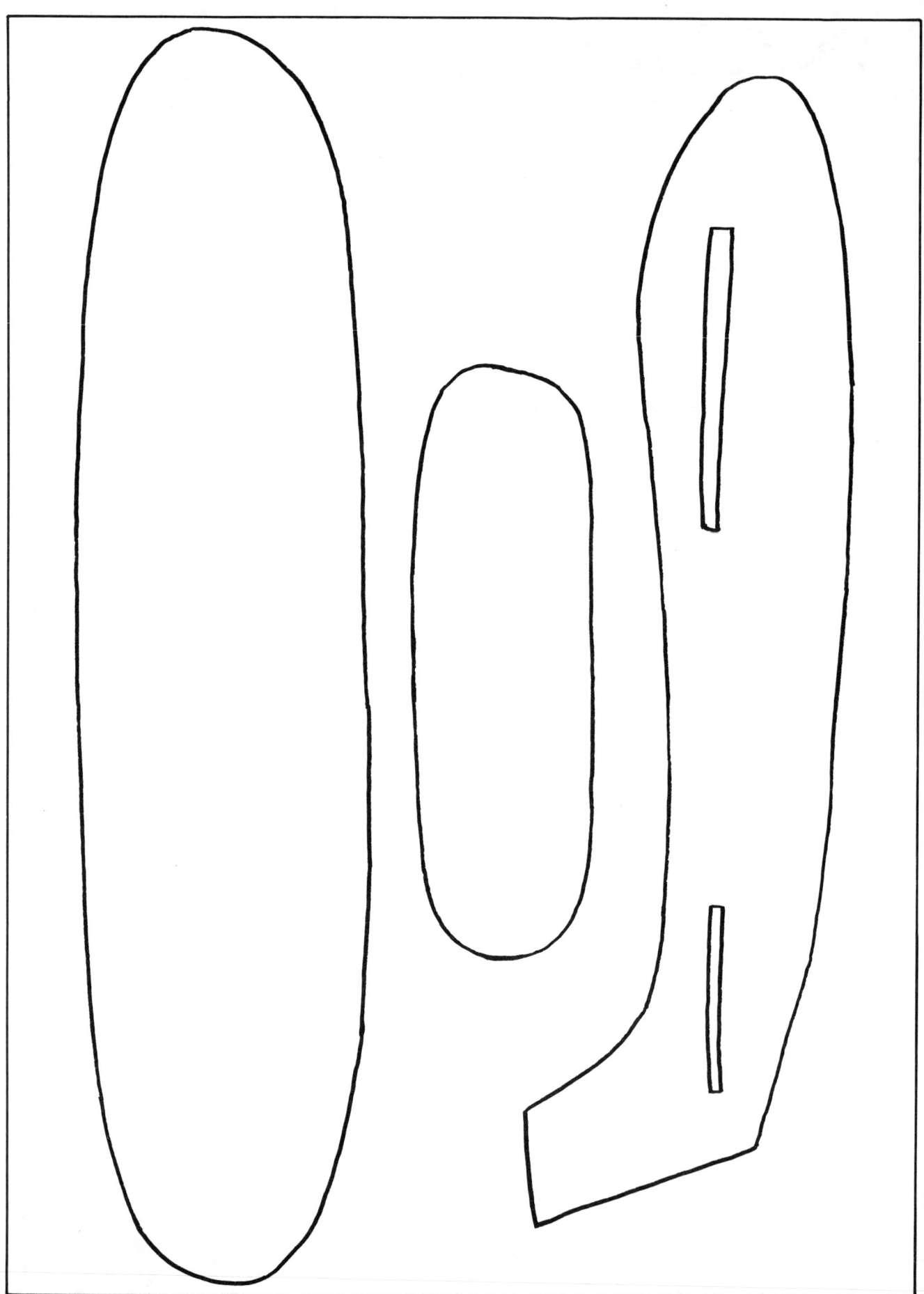

Grow Kit

WHAT YOU NEED:
Plastic ice cream bucket
Newspaper
Large ziplock bag
Old spoon
Seeds
Craft sticks
Permanent marker

WHAT YOU DO:
1. Fold the newspaper and place it inside the ziplock bag to make a kneeling pad. Close the bag.
2. Dig holes in dirt for seeds with the old spoon.
3. Print seed names on craft sticks with permanent marker and mark seed rows with them.
4. Fill the ice cream bucket with water and gently water the seeds.
5. Store gardening tools in bucket when not in use.

Headphones

WHAT YOU NEED:
Margarine tub
Kitchen shears
2 plastic refill cups
Paper punch
2 brass paper fasteners

WHAT YOU DO:
1. Cut off ¾" from the top of the margarine tub. Save this curved plastic strip.
2. Punch a hole in each end of the strip.
3. Punch a hole in the rim of each plastic refill cup.
4. Attach the plastic cups to the strip with brass paper fasteners.

Hug Me

WHAT YOU NEED:
Odd sock
Polyester stuffing
Permanent marker
Yarn (optional)

WHAT YOU DO:
1. Stuff the foot end of the sock with polyester.
2. Knot the open end of the sock.
3. Draw a face on the sock with marker. Add yarn trim if desired.

Jump Rope

WHAT YOU NEED:
Kitchen shears
Length of old clothesline
2 spools (same size)

WHAT YOU DO:
1. Cut a piece of clothesline long enough for a jump rope. Test to see if it swings over a child's head.
2. Make a knot on each side of the rope ten inches from the end.
3. Slip a spool handle onto each end, pushing it up to knot.
4. Knot the rope ends to keep the handles in place.

Kitchen Caper

WHAT YOU NEED:
2 small margarine tubs
Scissors
2 straight wooden clothespins
2 plastic picnic spoons

WHAT YOU DO:
1. Cut the top half off one tub to make a frying pan.
2. Cut a small hole in the side of each tub just big enough to hold the clothespin tops.
3. Push the top of a clothespin through each hole to make handles for the frying pan and saucepan.
4. Use the picnic spoons for stirring.

Knee Desk

WHAT YOU NEED:
Piece of corrugated cardboard
Long envelope
White glue
String
Scissors
Nail or nutpick
Pencil

WHAT YOU DO:
1. Cut the flap off the envelope.
2. Glue the envelope to the lower edge of the cardboard.
3. Fill the envelope with letter-writing supplies.
4. Poke a hole in an upper corner of the cardboard with a nail or nutpick.
5. Cut a piece of string about two feet long. Tie one end to the cardboard and the other end to the pencil to complete the knee desk.

Marble Maze

WHAT YOU NEED:
Large margarine tub with lid
Permanent marker
Ball-point pen
Penny
Small scissors
Small marble

WHAT YOU DO:
1. Draw a spiral on the lid with permanent marker.
2. Trace around the penny with a ball-point pen at three places along the spiral and in the center of the lid.
3. Cut out the traced circles and the spiral.
4. Snap the lid on the tub.
5. Start the marble rolling around the maze. Try to get it around the spiral without falling into the tub.

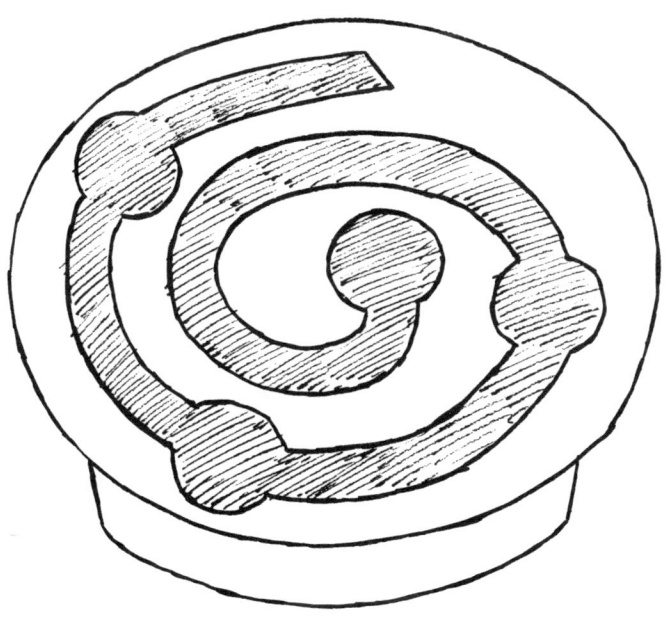

Mini Greenhouse

WHAT YOU NEED:
Largest size clear plastic pop bottle
Kitchen shears
Aluminum pot pie pan
Seeds
Dirt

WHAT YOU DO:
1. Carefully cut off the bottom part of the pop bottle.
2. Rinse and dry this dome to make the greenhouse window.
3. Fill the pot pie pan with dirt.
4. Plant seeds in the dirt. (Seeds can be purchased or saved from fruits and vegetables.)
5. Gently water the seeds.
6. Place the greenhouse window over the pan. Leave it in place until the plants touch the top.

Moon People

WHAT YOU NEED:
Spring-type clothespins
Plastic egg (from pantyhose)
Permanent marker

WHAT YOU DO:
1. Snap three clothespins onto one half of a plastic egg. Repeat with the other half.
2. Draw faces with permanent marker.

Party Pak

WHAT YOU NEED:
Sunday comics
Scissors
White glue
Paper lunch bags
Toilet paper tubes
Small prizes
Paper napkins
Paper plates
Balloons

WHAT YOU DO:
1. Cut out pictures from the comics. Glue one picture on each paper lunch bag to make party bags.
2. Put a small prize inside each tube. Cut comics to fit around tubes, leaving ends long. Glue comics to tubes, then twist paper ends closed.
3. Fold full-page comics into paper party hats.
4. Gather paper plates, napkins, balloons, bags, tubes, and hats together. Add a snack to complete the party pak.

Pencil Pinwheel

WHAT YOU NEED:
1 piece of colored paper
Scissors
Pushpin with plastic top
Unsharpened pencil with eraser

WHAT YOU DO:
1. Trim the paper into a square. Fold the square in half along the diagonal. Unfold, then fold again along the other diagonal. Open up the paper.
2. Cut along the fold lines, stopping just before the center.
3. Bend the four corners of the paper toward the center into a pinwheel. Poke the pushpin through the corners and the center of the paper into the eraser of the pencil. Make sure the pinwheel can spin.
4. Blow on the pinwheel or let the wind whirl it around.

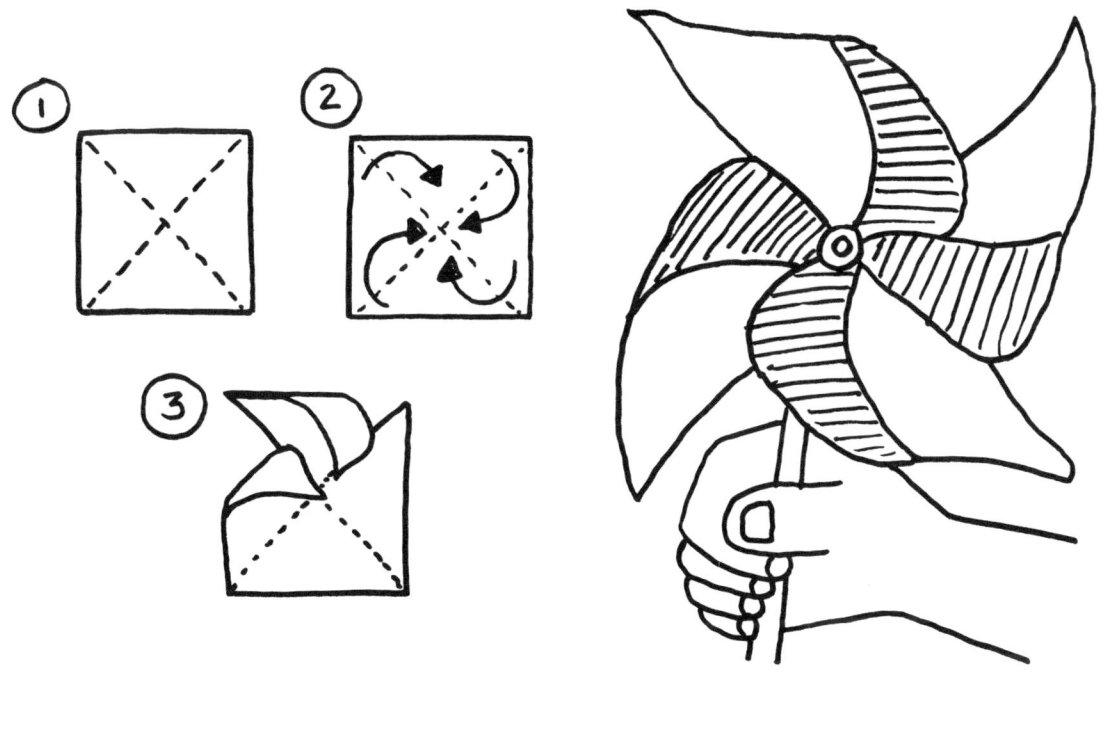

Pick Up Picks

WHAT YOU NEED:
Colored toothpicks
Margarine tub with lid
Pencil
Paper

WHAT YOU DO:
1. Fill the margarine tub with colored toothpicks.
2. Shake the tub and scatter the picks.
3. Play like Pick Up Sticks. Keep score with pencil and paper. Count four points for red, three points for yellow, two points for green, one point for blue. Player with the highest score wins.

Pilot Control Panel

WHAT YOU NEED:
Large piece of cardboard
Paper plate
4 plastic lids
5 notched plastic trash bag ties
5 brass paper fasteners
Nail or nutpick
Permanent marker
Scissors

WHAT YOU DO:
1. Poke holes in the paper plate and plastic lids with a nail or nutpick. Arrange on cardboard, then poke holes through it.
2. Attach paper plate to cardboard with a brass paper fastener to make the steering wheel.
3. Print N, S, E, W on one plastic lid for the compass. Print clock numerals on the second lid. Print engine speed numerals on the third lid. Print altitude numerals on the fourth lid.
4. Trim the trash bag ties to look like dial hands. Cut the dial hands to fit the lids.
5. Push a brass fastener through each trash bag tie and each lid. Then attach all dials to the cardboard control panel.

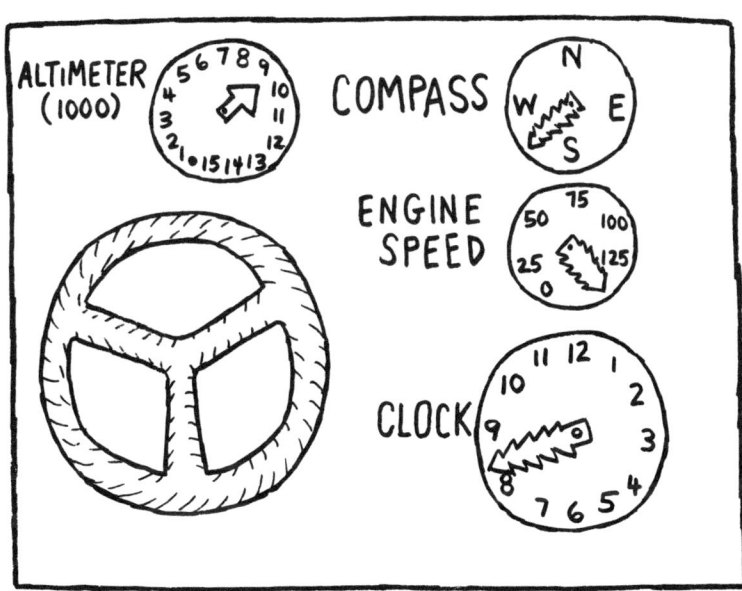

Plain Plane

WHAT YOU NEED:
Plastic detergent bottle with top
Kitchen shears
3 plastic bottle tops (same size)
2 pipe cleaners
Large plastic lids
Nail
Brass paper fastener

WHAT YOU DO:
1. Screw the top on the detergent bottle. Cut a hole in one side of the bottle to make the cockpit.
2. Cut any shape propeller, wing, and tail from plastic lids.
3. Carefully cut two slits beneath the cockpit hole, one on each side of the plane. Push the wing through these slits to form the cockpit slits. Fasten the tail to the back in the same way.
4. Poke a hole in the center of the propeller. Poke a matching hole in the front of the plane with a nail. Fasten the propeller to the plane with the brass paper fastener.
5. Poke holes in the bottle where wheels are to go. Attach the wheels with pipe cleaners, pushing them through the bottle and bending the ends to keep the wheels in place.
6. Fly plain planes on fantasy adventures.

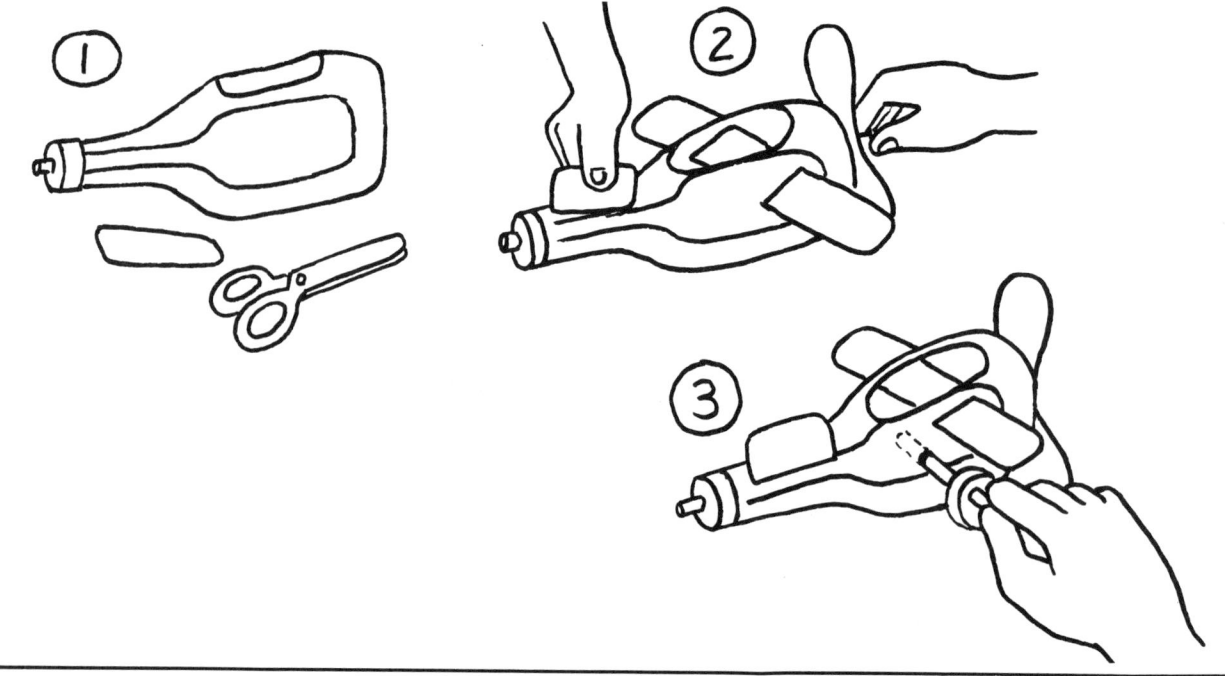

Pop Bop

WHAT YOU NEED:
Largest size plastic pop bottle
4 plastic lids
Permanent marker
Spongy ball

WHAT YOU DO:
1. Number the lids with permanent marker to make baseball bases.
2. Set out the bases in a safe place to play.
3. Follow the rules for baseball and hit the spongy ball with the pop bottle bat.

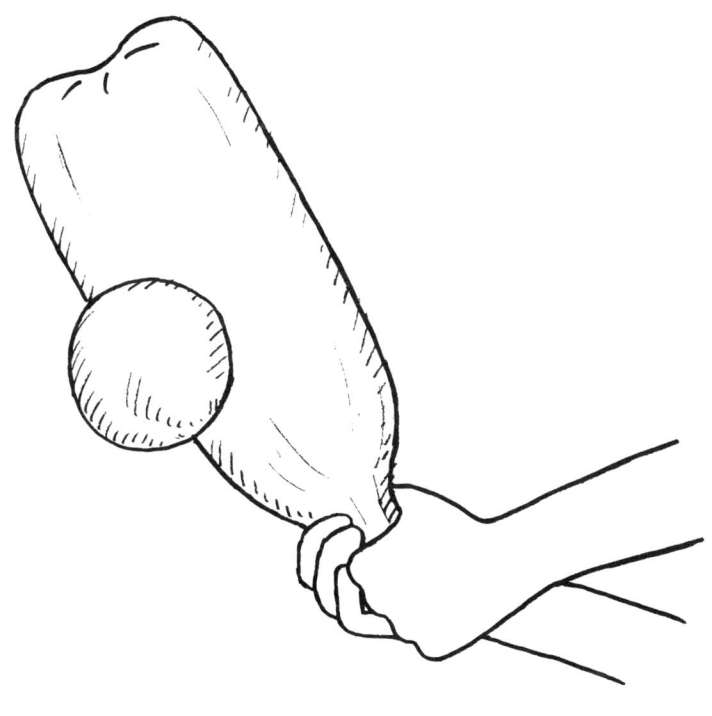

Pop Goes the Clown's Nose!

WHAT YOU NEED:
Paper plate
Crayon
Nail or nutpick
Balloons
Tape
Pushpins (with plastic tops)
Blindfold

WHAT YOU DO:
1. Draw a clown face on the paper plate. Omit the nose.
2. Poke a hole in the center of the plate with a nail or nutpick.
3. Blow up the balloon. Knot the end tightly, push it through the hole in the plate, and tape it securely to the back to make the clown nose.
4. Tack the clown on the wall and play like "Pin the Tail on the Donkey." Blindfolded players try to pop the clown's nose with pushpins.

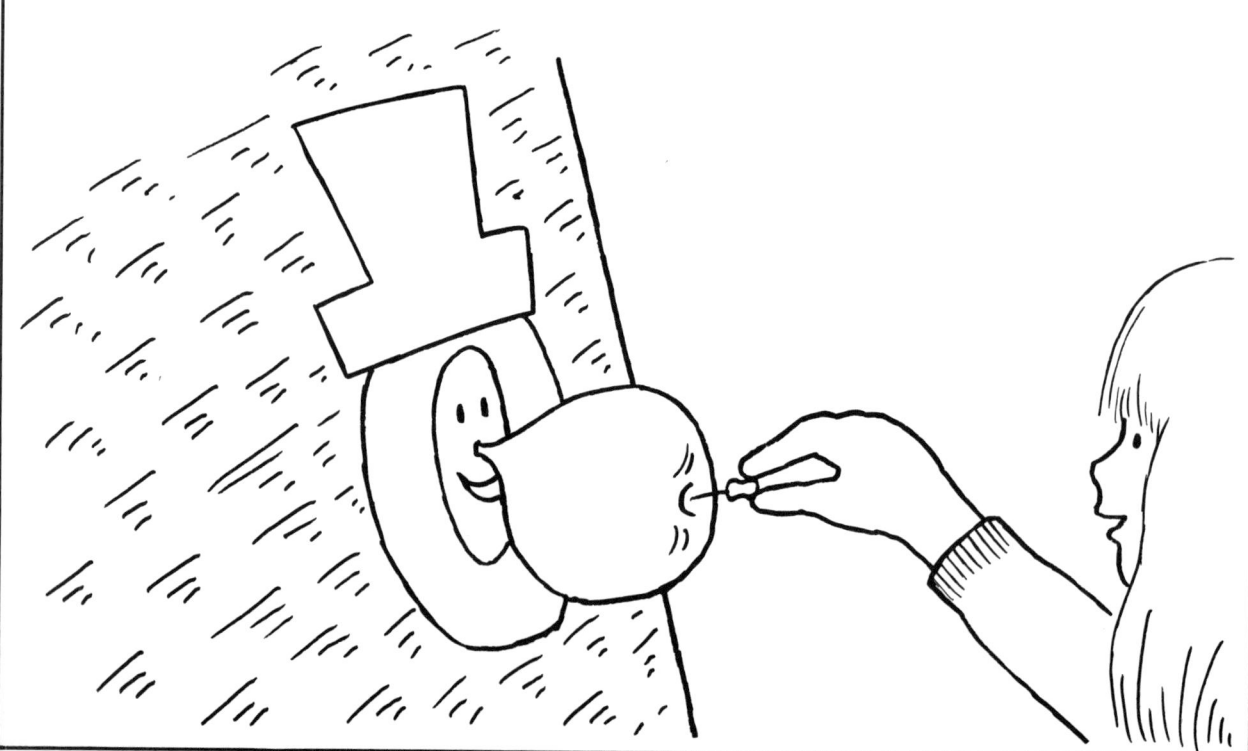

Rack 'Em, Stack 'Em

WHAT YOU NEED:
Large lids from peel-top juice cans
Potato chip cannister
Colored paper
Scissors
White glue

WHAT YOU DO:
1. Save lots of clean juice can lids.
2. Cut colored paper to fit around the potato chip cannister and glue it on.
3. Fill the cannister with the lids.
4. Use the lids to stack into tall towers, make alphabet letters, or all sorts of shapes on the floor.

Rainbow Book

WHAT YOU NEED:
Colored paper
String
Old magazines
Scissors
Paste

WHAT YOU DO:
1. Stack several pieces of colored paper about the size of this book in a pile. Fold the pile in half.
2. Tie a string or a piece of yarn around the fold to make a book.
3. Cut out magazine pictures with lots of different colors.
4. Paste pictures on the matching colored paper page. Tell rainbow stories to go with the pictures.

Rocket

WHAT YOU NEED:
Potato chip cannister
Aluminum foil
3 spring-type clothespins
Coffee can lid (2-pound size)
Pencil
Paper
Scissors
Tape

WHAT YOU DO:
1. Wrap the cannister with foil, tucking ends into the opening and taping in place.
2. Snap the clothespins onto the opening to make the rocket stand.
3. Trace around the coffee can lid on paper. Cut out this circle and make a slit halfway through its diameter.
4. Bend the circle into a cone and tape the ends in place.
5. Tape the cone to the top of the cannister.

Royal Guard

WHAT YOU NEED:
Spring-type wooden clothespins
Small pipe cleaners
Cotton balls
White glue

WHAT YOU DO:
1. Twist a pipe cleaner around the narrow end of a clothespin.
2. Bend in the pipe cleaner ends for hands.
3. Glue a cotton ball on top of the narrow end of the clothespin to make the guard's fur hat.

Small Stuff

WHAT YOU NEED:
Margarine tubs
Cardboard box bottom
Doublestick tape

WHAT YOU DO:
1. Fit clean tubs into the box bottom. Tape in place, if you like.
2. Store small things such as shells, rocks, stamps, buttons, and marbles in the tubs to prevent loss.

Soap Boat

WHAT YOU NEED:
Bar of Ivory soap
Plastic coffee can lid
Ball-point pen
Scissors
Paper punch
Plastic straw

WHAT YOU DO:
1. Trace the sail pattern onto the plastic lid with the ball-point pen and cut out.
2. Punch two holes in the sail as shown.
3. Cut the straw in half. Use one half as a mast, pushing it through the holes in the sail.
4. Slowly stick the straw mast into the center of the bar of soap and set it in the water.

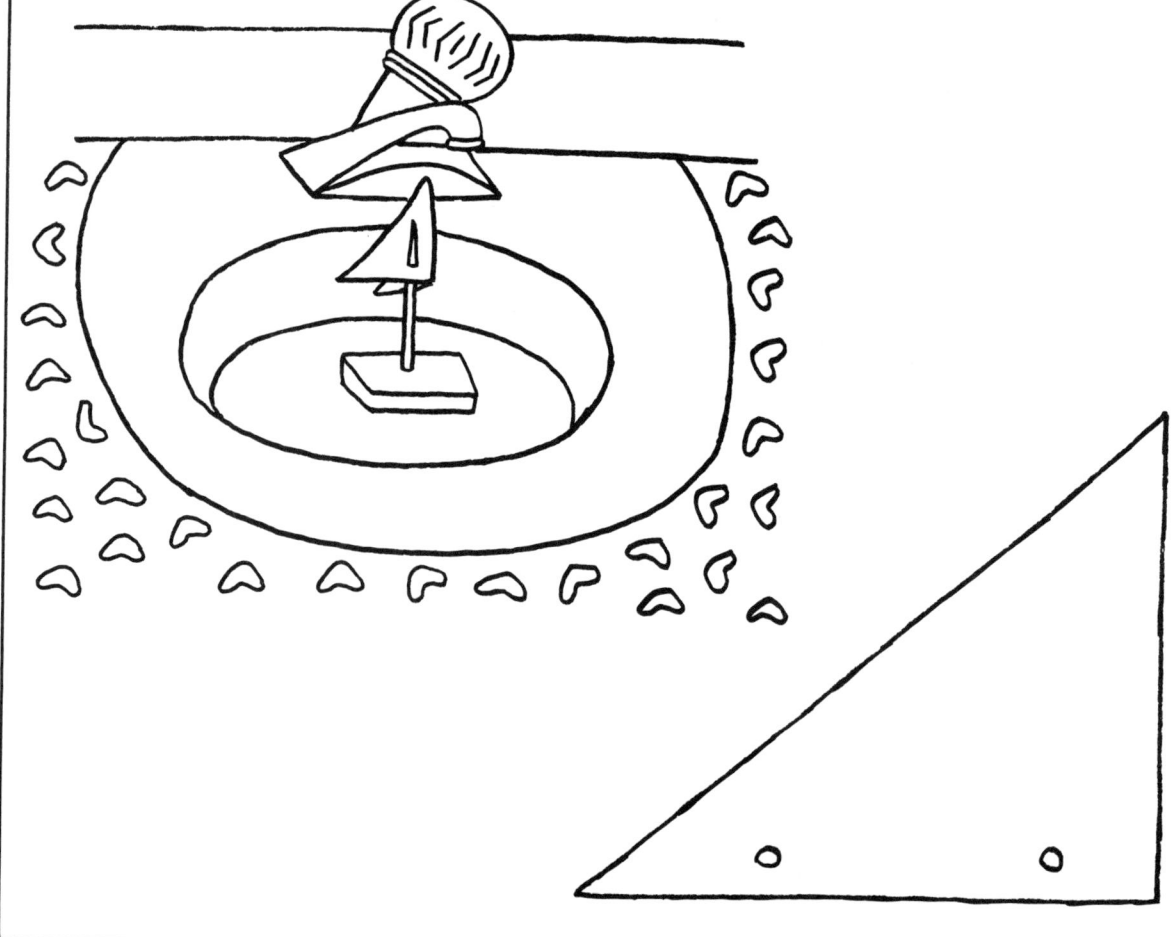

Spongy Blocks

WHAT YOU NEED:
Inexpensive sponges
Plastic bucket

WHAT YOU DO:
1. Store sponges in the bucket.
2. Use sponges as building blocks. When they are knocked down, they fall without a sound.

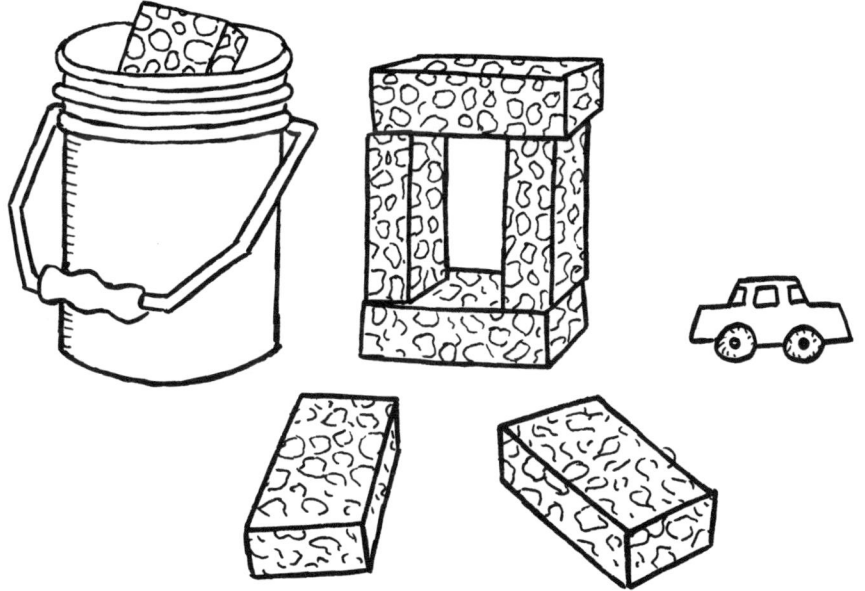

Squirt Tricks

WHAT YOU NEED:
Dishwashing liquid bottles (1 per person)
Craft sticks (1 per person)
Permanent marker

WHAT YOU DO:
1. Rinse and drain the bottles to get all the soap out.
2. Print each player's name on a craft stick to make a squirt marker.
3. Fill bottles with water and replace caps.
4. Draw a starting line on the ground in a safe, open space. Players stand behind the starting line and see who can squirt the farthest. Players use squirt markers to identify their shots.
5. Players can also squirt out their names, draw pictures with water, and shoot at targets.

Stencils and Pencils

WHAT YOU NEED:
Cookie cutters
Pencils
Index cards
Scissors
Paper

WHAT YOU DO:
1. Trace around a cookie cutter on a file card.
2. Cut out the cookie shape, saving the frame to make a stencil.
3. Trace a different cookie cutter on each card.
4. Use stencils and pencils to make pictures on paper. Colored pencils add to the fun.

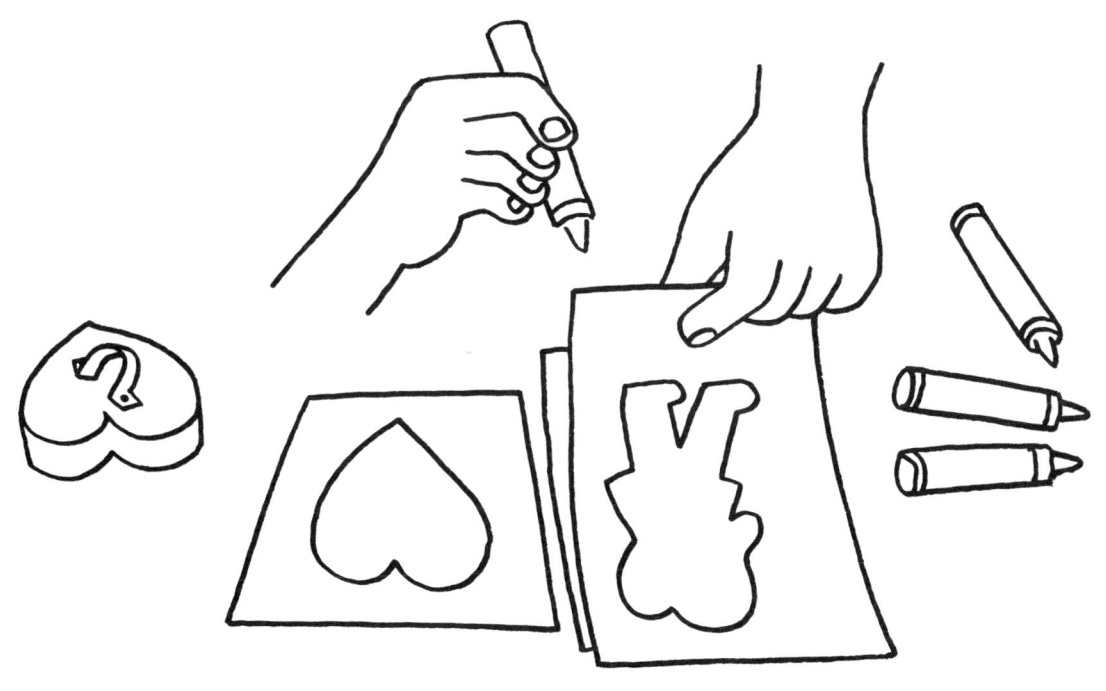

Stone Age Jewelry

WHAT YOU NEED:
Drinking straws
Scissors
Plastic lid (colored, if possible)
Ball-point pen
Paper punch
Needle with a large eye
Yarn

WHAT YOU DO:
1. Cut the straws into one-inch lengths.
2. Draw animal teeth (shaped like large apostrophes) on the plastic lid with ball-point pen.
3. Cut out the tooth shapes and punch one hole in each.
4. Thread the needle with enough yarn for a necklace.
5. String tooth shapes and straws alternately on the yarn. Tie the ends together to complete the necklace.
6. Make a stone age bracelet in the same way with a shorter length of yarn.

Teddy's Picnic

WHAT YOU NEED:
4 plastic milk bottle tops
4 toothpaste tops
4 ice cream tasting spoons
Plastic berry basket
Pipe cleaner
Fabric scrap
Ruler
Pencil
Pinking shears

WHAT YOU DO:
1. Fasten the pipe cleaner to the berry basket to make a handle for Teddy's picnic basket.
2. Draw two squares on the fabric and cut out.
3. Put one square of fabric into the basket for a picnic cloth. Cut the other square into four small squares and fold for napkins.
4. Pack the picnic basket with napkins, bottle top plates, toothpaste top glasses, and the little tasting spoons.

Tip Tops

WHAT YOU NEED:
Plastic milk bottle tops
Small nail or nutpick
Round toothpicks

WHAT YOU DO:
1. Poke a hole in the center of each bottle top with a nail or nutpick.
2. Push a toothpick through each bottle top. Place the bottle top about two-thirds of the way down the toothpick.
3. Spin the tops and see which one spins the longest.

Toy Town

WHAT YOU NEED:
Cardboard
Marker
Old magazines
Scissors
White glue
Small cars and trucks

WHAT YOU DO:
1. Draw streets, parking spaces, railroad tracks, a pond, and other elements of a town on the cardboard.
2. Cut out magazine pictures of houses and buildings to go with the town and glue in place.
3. Add small cars and trucks and the toy town is ready for play.

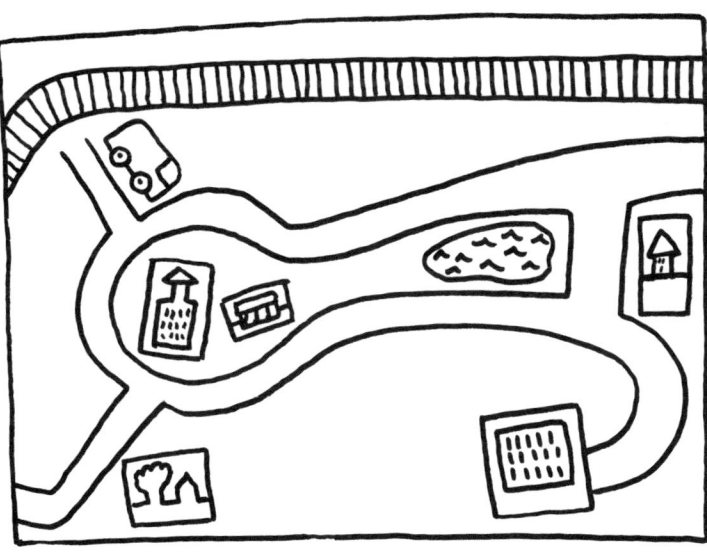

Triangle Tents

WHAT YOU NEED:
Big refrigerator box (free from appliance store)
Permanent markers or paint
Knife

WHAT YOU DO:
1. Cut the refrigerator box in half lengthwise to make two triangles.
2. Stand the triangles up like tents and decorate with permanent markers or paint.

T V Me

WHAT YOU NEED:
Large tissue box
Brown paper bag
Pencil
Scissors
Glue
Marker
Small mirror
Doublestick tape

WHAT YOU DO:
1. Trace the box bottom and one long side on the paper bag and cut out.
2. Stand the tissue box on its side. Glue the largest rectangle on the bottom and the other on the top.
3. Draw a television screen and control knobs on the box with marker.
4. Tape the mirror to the center of the television screen.
5. Hold the box up and perform into it.

U.S. Mail

WHAT YOU NEED:
Large brown paper bag
Crayons
Paper punch
Scissors
String
Empty envelopes, old postcards

WHAT YOU DO:
1. Color red, white, and blue stripes on one side of the bag and print U.S. Mail on the other side.
2. Fold down a rim on the bag and punch holes on the shorter sides.
3. Cut about two feet of string and tie through the holes in the rim for a handle.
4. Fill the bag with empty envelopes and old postcards.

Wash-Me Mitt

WHAT YOU NEED:
Old washcloth
Scissors
Needle
Thread
Yarn
Permanent marker

WHAT YOU DO:
1. Cut the washcloth in half. Fold one piece in half and stitch around two open sides, curving up toward the folded top.
2. Loop yarn to make fringe along the top of the wash-me mitt and stitch it in place if hair is desired.
3. Draw a face on the mitt with the permanent marker.
4. Repeat the procedure with the other half of the washcloth to make a second mitt.

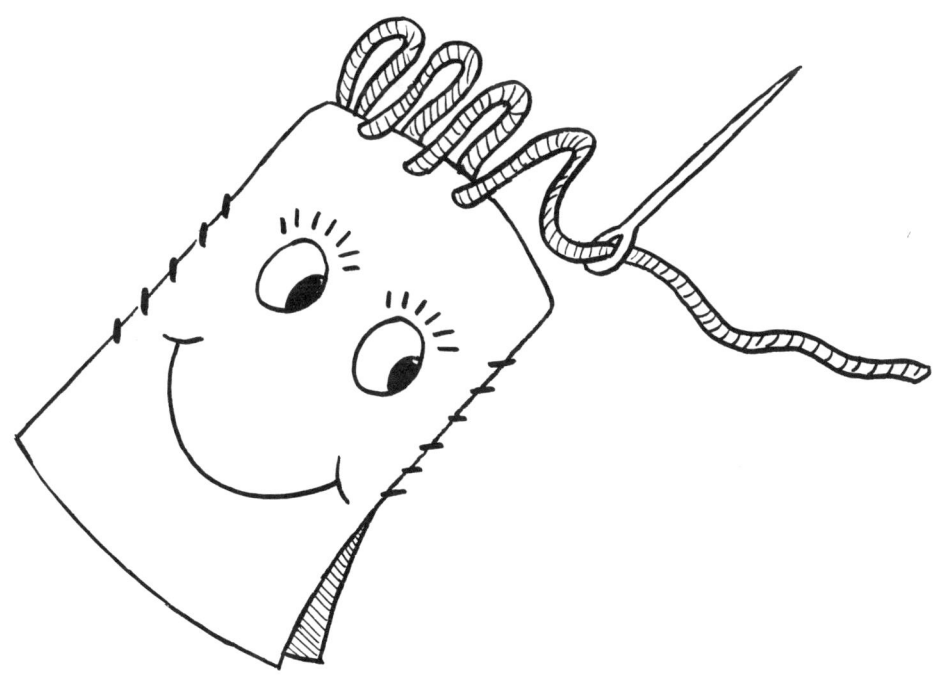

Wind Chimes

WHAT YOU NEED:
Old silverware (no sharp edges)
String
Scissors
Wire hanger (slacks type)

WHAT YOU DO:
1. Cut a length of string for each piece of silverware.
2. Tie the strings onto the silverware and then onto the hanger. Check to see that the strings hang evenly.
3. Hang the wind chimes outdoors to hear forks and spoons make music in the breeze.

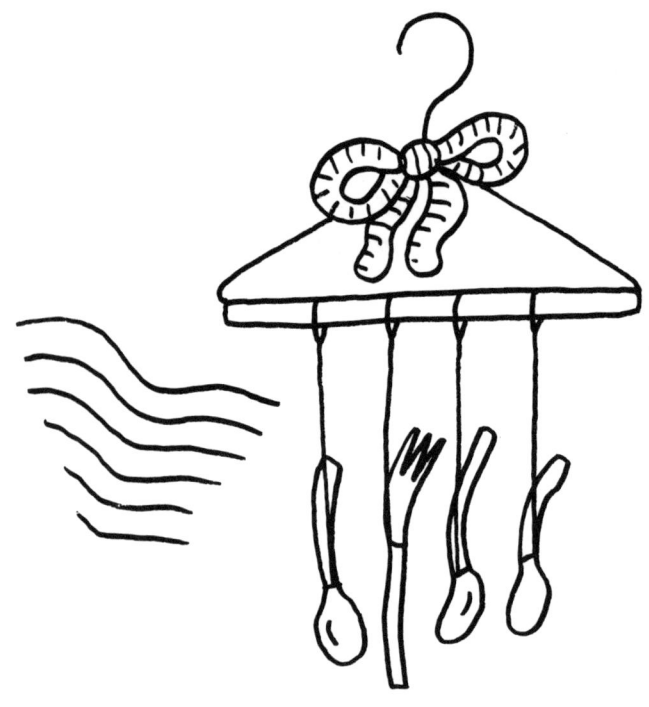

Windsock

WHAT YOU NEED:
Paper bag
Crayons
Scissors
String
White glue
Tape

WHAT YOU DO:
1. Fold a rim around the top of the bag, turning it to the outside.
2. Draw pictures on both sides of the bag.
3. Cut a length of string to fit around the top of the bag. Place the string under the rim and glue in place.
4. Cut another piece of string for a handle and tape it to the top of the bag.
5. When the glue is dry, pull it along and let it fill with air.

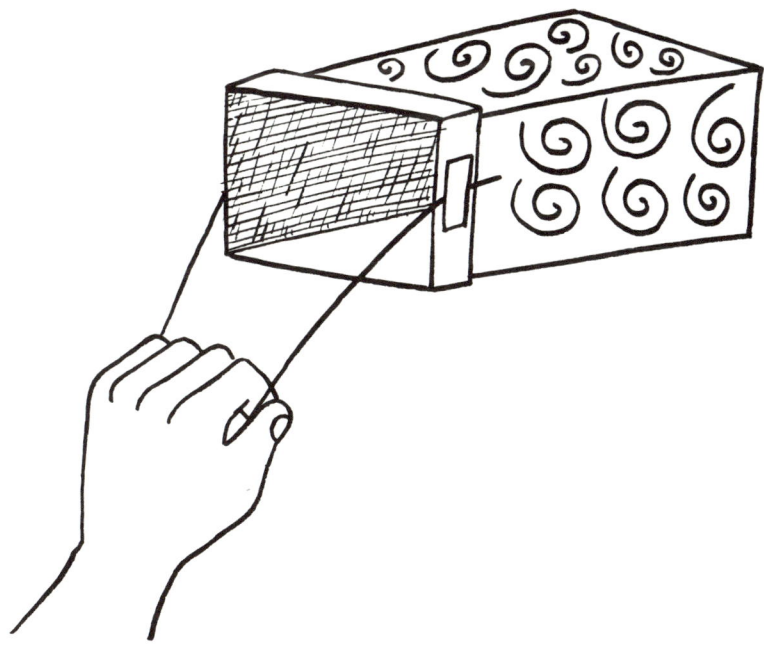

Wooden Spoon Doll

WHAT YOU NEED:
Permanent marker
Wooden spoon
Yarn
Scissors
White glue
Handkerchief or cloth

WHAT YOU DO:
1. Draw a face on the bowl of the spoon.
2. Cut lengths of yarn and tie in the middle to make the part in the doll's hair.
3. Glue the hair on the spoon, spreading it out a bit to cover the wood.
4. Cut a small hole in the center of the handkerchief or cloth.
5. Slip the fabric onto the spoon handle and tie it in place with yarn.

Wristwatch

WHAT YOU NEED:
Plastic milk bottle top
Nail or nutpick
Fine-point permanent marker
2 notched plastic trash bag ties
Small brass paper fastener
Small paper clip
Scissors

WHAT YOU DO:
1. Poke a hole in the center of the bottle top with a nail or nutpick.
2. Draw hour lines around the edge of the bottle top with marker.
3. Slip the point of one trash bag tie through the hole in the other to link the two together.
4. Assemble the watch by putting the brass paper fastener through the paper clip, then through the bottle top, and lastly through the joint of the trash bag ties. Use the other point and hole apparatus to fit the watch to its wearer.

Yolk-O-Motion

WHAT YOU NEED:
Plastic egg with 2 halves (from pantyhose or Easter egg)
Weight (small rock, washer, etc.)
Heavy tape
Permanent marker

WHAT YOU DO:
1. Put a weight in the small half of the egg. Use a small rock or plumbing washer or anything else that will balance the egg. Experiment until the weight works properly.
2. Center the weight and tape it in place.
3. Put the two halves of the egg together. Tape egg closed for smaller children.
4. Draw a face on the egg with marker.
5. Set the egg in motion by spinning it, rocking it, or flicking it with a finger. The egg will bounce back up again.

4302-10
5-33